FASTEN YOUR SEATBELT

Stats and facts • Top makes • Top models • Top speeds

By David Kimber, Bill Gunston, Jeff Painter and Steve Parker

Studio Manager: Sara Greasley
Editor: Claire Lucas
Production Controller: Ed Green
Production Manager: Suzy Kelly

ISBN-13: 978-1-84898-080-8 pbk
This revised edition published in 2009 by *ticktock Media* Ltd

Printed in China
9 8 7 6 5 4 3 2 1

A CIP catalogue record for this book is available from the British Library.
All rights reserved. No part of this publication may be reproduced, copied, stored in a retrieval system or transmitted in any form or by any means electronic, mechanical, photocopying, recording or otherwise without prior written permission of the copyright owner.

Copyright © *ticktock* Entertainment Ltd 2006
First published in Great Britain in 2006 as *Amazing Machines* by *ticktock Media* Ltd,
The Old Sawmill, 103 Goods Station Road, Tunbridge Wells, Kent TN1 2DP

Picture credits
(t =top, b=bottom, c=centre, l=left, r=right OFC=outside front cover, OBC=outside back cover):
Shutterstock: OFC. Cars: All images Car Photo Library-www.carphoto.co.uk, except Alamy: 8–9c. Planes: Corbis: 28–29, 46–47. Aviation Picture Library: 30–31, 32–33, 36–37, 38-39, 40–41. Lockheed: 42–43, OBC. NASA: 34–35, 44–45, 48–49. Motorbikes: All images Car Photo Library – www.carphoto.co.uk, except Hwithaar/Wikimedia Commons: 50-51c. Boats: Alamy: 85. Beken of Cowes: 76c, 82–83c. British Antarctic Survey: 78–79. Corbis: 74–75c, 80–81, 83t, 84c. John Clark Photography: 72–73c. Hawkes Ocean Technologies: 75t. RNLI: 90–91. World of Residensea: 88–89. Yamaha: 87t.

Every effort has been made to trace copyright holders, and we apologize in advance for any omissions. We would be pleased to insert the appropriate acknowledgments in any subsequent edition of this publication.

The publishers would like to thank Keith Faulkner of *Jane's Defence Weekly*, Richard Newland of *Fast Bikes* magazine, Jamie Asher, Sam Petter and Tim Bones.

CONTENTS

Unless otherwise stated, the cost quoted refers to the time of the machine's launch.

Introduction

CARS

The fastest cars have room for a driver, passenger and not much else! These machines are certainly not sensible family cars – they are built for speed. They are low to the ground with an **aerodynamic** body and a powerful engine. Sports cars are admired all over the world. They are not just beautiful pieces of engineering, they are works of art.

PLANES

The first plane flew in 1903. Aviation technology developed quickly, and now millions of passengers travel by plane each year. Planes are flying faster and further than ever before. Today, some of the most exciting new aircraft are being developed by the military.

SUPERBIKES

Motorbikes have always symbolized the freedom of the road and an escape from everyday life. The machines in this book would make that escape easier than ever before. They are some of the fastest bikes in production. These are not just motorbikes, they are **superbikes.**

BOATS

All boats float on water, have a means of power and a way for the crew to control speed and direction. But the variation in boat design is immense. Some are built for short journeys in safe waters, while others brave the worst weather on the open sea. The boats in this book celebrate the amazing diversity of travel by water.

ASTON MARTIN V12 VANQUISH

The British firm Aston Martin made their first sports car back in 1914. Nearly 90 years later the **V12** Vanquish went on sale. With a powerful **engine** and a **body** made out of the lightweight metal **aluminium**, the four-seater Vanquish is one of the fastest cars in the world.

DID YOU KNOW?

In the film Die Another Day, *the super spy James Bond drives a V12 Vanquish.*

The car has **tyre** pressure sensors, rain sensors and even sensors that switch the headlights on when it gets too dark.

The V12 has **Formula One**-style **gearchange paddles** behind the steering wheel. You click right to change up a **gear** and left to change down.

STATS AND FACTS

LAUNCHED: *2001*

ORIGIN: *UK*

ENGINE: *5,935* **cc** *V12, front-mounted*

MAX POWER: *343* **kW** *(460* **bhp***) at 6,800* **rpm**

MAX TORQUE: *540* **Nm** *(400* **ft lb***) at 5,500 rpm*

MAX SPEED: *306 km/h (190 mph)*

ACCELERATION: *0–97 km/h (0–60 mph): 4.5 seconds*

WEIGHT: *1.83 tonnes*

COST: *£158,000*

The body panels are shaped by hand to make sure the edges are perfect.

BMW Z8

The Z8 is a modern sports car with old fashioned looks. This **roadster** is based on the beautiful BMW 507 built in the 1950s. Thanks to the enormous power from its **V8** engine, the Z8 is more than just beautiful. Without the electronic speed reducer the top speed would be 290 km/h (180 mph).

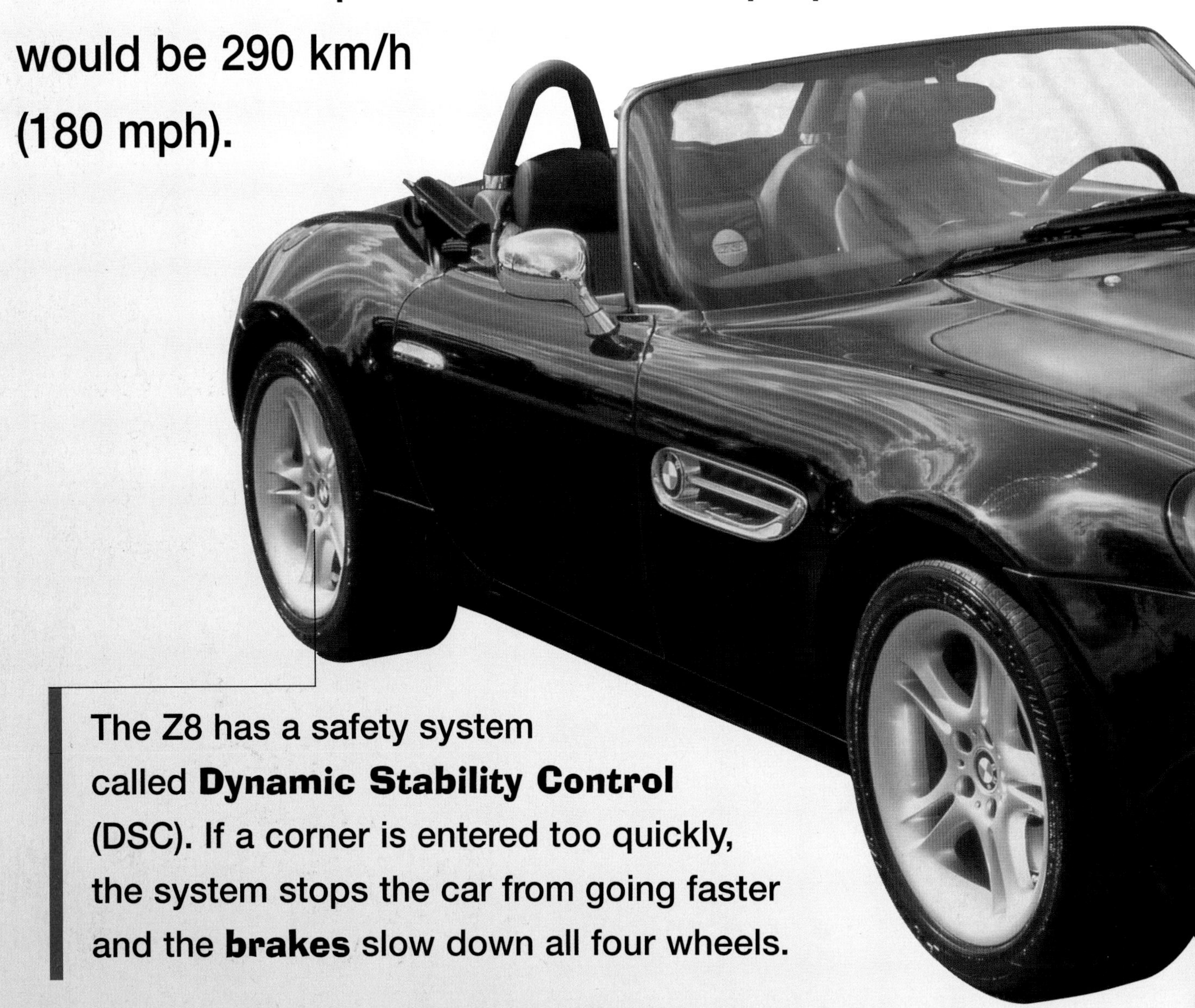

The Z8 has a safety system called **Dynamic Stability Control** (DSC). If a corner is entered too quickly, the system stops the car from going faster and the **brakes** slow down all four wheels.

The dials are unusually placed in the centre of the **dashboard**. This gives the driver a clear view of the road.

STATS AND FACTS

LAUNCHED: *2000*

ORIGIN: *Germany*

ENGINE: *4,941 cc 32-***valve** *V8, front-mounted*

MAX POWER: *298 kW (400 bhp) at 6,600 rpm*

MAX TORQUE: *500 Nm (369 ft lb) at 3,800 rpm*

MAX SPEED: *250 km/h (155 mph) (limited)*

ACCELERATION: *0–97 km/h (0–60 mph): 4.8 seconds*

WEIGHT: *1.58 tonnes*

COST: *£85,000*

Z8 customers could choose between a hard top or a soft top for their roadster.

DID YOU KNOW?

The Z8's* satellite navigation *system is hidden behind a flap in the dashboard.

BUGATTI VEYRON

The Bugatti Veyron is one of the most expensive **production cars** in the world, and one of the fastest. When the Veyron reaches 220 km/h (137 mph) hydraulics lower the car and its rear retractable spoiler and wing are **deployed** to help hold it to the road.

The initials 'EB' on the Bugatti badge stand for Ettore Bugatti, the founder of the company. The Veyron is named after Pierre Veyron, who won the 1939 24 Hours of Le Mans race for the original Bugatti firm.

A unique aluminium alloy was developed for the interior of the Veyron to ensure that it remains shiny.

The Bugatti emblem in the large **radiator** grille is enamelled by hand.

STATS AND FACTS

LAUNCHED: *2005*

ORIGIN: *Built in France*

ENGINE: *7,993 cc, 64 valve, mid-mounted, quad turbo engine*

MAX POWER: *736 kW (1,001 bhp)*

MAX TORQUE: *1,250 Nm (922 ft lb) at 2,200–5,500 rpm*

MAX SPEED: *407.5 km/h (253.2 mph)*

ACCELERATION:
0–100 km/h (0–62 mph): 2.5 seconds
0–400 km/h (0–249 mph): 55.6 seconds

WEIGHT: *1.888 tonnes*

COST: *£840,000*

DID YOU KNOW?

The Veyron was the world's fastest production car, until the Shelby SSC Ultimate Aero TT reached 412.28 km/h (256.18 mph) in 1997.

CHEVROLET CORVETTE Z06

The American car manufacturer Chevrolet built their first Corvette in 1953. It soon became the world's most popular sports car. Millions of Corvettes have been sold all over the world.

The reason for the car's success is simple. The Corvette is very fast but comes at a reasonable price.

DID YOU KNOW?

Over 200 of the earliest Corvettes have survived. They are now highly collectable.

In 1999 Chevrolet gave the Corvette a fighter plane-style display. Speed, revolutions per minute (rpm) and fuel levels are projected onto the windscreen.

This beautiful Corvette was built in 1960. Its powerful V8 engine gave a top speed of 209 km/h (130 mph). The average top speed of cars at that time was just 80 km/h (50 mph).

STATS AND FACTS

LAUNCHED: *1997*

ORIGIN: *USA*

ENGINE: *5,666 cc V8, front-mounted*

MAX POWER: *287 kW (385 bhp) at 6,000 rpm*

MAX TORQUE: *521 Nm (385 ft lb) at 4,800 rpm*

MAX SPEED: *282 km/h (175 mph)*

ACCELERATION: *0–97 km/h (0–60 mph): 4 seconds*

WEIGHT: *1.41 tonnes*

COST: *£37,999*

The Corvette comes in three body styles: **coupé** (hard top) for cold-weather driving, **targa** (with solid lift-out roof panel) and **convertible** (soft top) for warm-weather driving.

FERRARI F50

Ferrari is one of the most famous makers of sports cars in the world. The F50 is one of the most exclusive models ever built. Just 349 cars were built to celebrate the Italian legend's 50th anniversary in 1995. This incredible car is powered by a slightly less powerful version of a 1990 Formula One engine.

The F50's body, doors and seats are made from lightweight **carbon fibre**.

Underneath the car the body is completely flat. The four **exhausts** stick out through holes cut into the rear, just like a racing car.

STATS AND FACTS

LAUNCHED: *1995*

ORIGIN: *Italy*

ENGINE: *4,699 cc 60-valve V12, mid-mounted*

MAX POWER: *383 kW (513 bhp) at 8,000 rpm*

MAX TORQUE: *470 Nm (347 ft lb) at 6,500 rpm*

MAX SPEED: *325 km/h (202 mph)*

ACCELERATION: *0–97 km/h (0–60 mph): 3.7 seconds*

WEIGHT: *1.23 tonnes*

COST: *£342,700*

The engine is in the middle of the F50. It powers the Ferrari to 97 km/h (60 mph) in under four seconds. The car goes from 0–161 km/h (0–100 mph) in just eight seconds and 0–241 km/h (0–150 mph) in 18 seconds.

DID YOU KNOW?

The F50 is a very expensive car. But you still have to wind the windows up and down by hand!

JAGUAR XJ220S

In the late 1980s, the British car maker Jaguar decided to build a **supercar**. They called it the XJ220. In 1992 the first models were delivered to customers, costing £415,000 each. Two years later, Jaguar produced an even faster, lighter and cheaper version of the car. It was called the XJ220S.

DID YOU KNOW?

In 1994 racing driver Martin Brundle reached 349 km/h (217 mph) in an XJ220S. At the time this was the fastest speed ever recorded by a road car.

The back of the car has an enormous wing. It stretches right across the body of one of the widest sports cars ever made.

The XJ220S was built by TWR (Tom Walkinshaw Racing). They based their design on the XJ220C cars that took part in the Le Mans race in France in 1993.

STATS AND FACTS

LAUNCHED: *1994*

ORIGIN: *UK*

ENGINE: *3,498 cc twin-turbo V6, mid-mounted*

MAX POWER: *507 kW (680 bhp) at 7,200 rpm*

MAX TORQUE: *714 Nm (527 ft lb) at 5,000 rpm*

MAX SPEED: *349 km/h (217 mph)*

ACCELERATION: *0–97 km/h (0–60 mph): 3.3 seconds*

WEIGHT: *1.08 tonnes*

COST: *£293,750*

The XJ220's aluminium body was replaced with carbon fibre to make the XJ220S even lighter. The power was also increased from 404 kW (542 bhp) to 507 kW (680 bhp).

LAMBORGHINI MURCIÉLAGO

Ferrucio Lamborghini was a millionaire tractor maker from northern Italy. Unhappy with the Ferrari he owned he decided he could build a better car himself. In 1966 Lamborghini made the first real supercar, the Miura. In 2001, the company started selling their tenth model, the Murciélago.

The roof and the doors of the Murciélago are made of steel. The rest of the car is made from carbon fibre.

DID YOU KNOW?

The Lamborghini badge features a charging bull, a symbol of both beauty and violence.

To reverse the Murciélago, most drivers flip open a door, and sit on the edge of the car. They can then look over their shoulder to see where they are going!

STATS AND FACTS

LAUNCHED: *2001*

ORIGIN: *Italy*

ENGINE: *6,192 cc V12, mid-mounted*

MAX POWER: *426 kW (571 bhp) at 7,500 rpm*

MAX TORQUE: *649 Nm (479 ft lb) at 5,400 rpm*

MAX SPEED: *330 km/h (205 mph)*

ACCELERATION: *0–97 km/h (0–60 mph): 4 seconds*

WEIGHT: *1.65 tonnes*

COST: *£163,000*

The Murciélago is easier to drive than previous Lamborghinis. It has **four-wheel drive** and a safety system that slows the car down if it starts to lose its grip on the road.

McLAREN F1

McLaren are famous makers of **Formula One** cars. In 1992 the firm decided to make the ultimate supercar. The result was the F1. It was the first car costing one million dollars, and the fastest car on the road.

DID YOU KNOW?

An annual service for the McLaren F1 costs an amazing £25,000!

The back of the car is taken up by the huge BMW engine. It powers the F1 to 161 km/h (100 mph) two seconds faster than a Ferrari, and on to a blistering 386 km/h (240 mph).

STATS AND FACTS

LAUNCHED: *1992*

ORIGIN: *UK*

ENGINE: *6,064 cc 48-valve V12, mid-mounted*

MAX POWER: *468 kW (627 bhp) at 7,400 rpm*

MAX TORQUE: *649 Nm (479 ft lb) at 7,000 rpm*

MAX SPEED: *386.4 km/h (240.1 mph)*

ACCELERATION:
0–97 km/h (0–60 mph): 3.2 seconds
0–161 km/h (0–100 mph): 6.3 seconds

WEIGHT: *1.14 tonnes*

COST: *£634,500*

The F1's central driving position is unusual for a supercar. The two rear seats are also unusual for a sports car.

A total of 106 F1 road cars were built before McLaren stopped making them in 1998. Each one took nearly two months to build!

PAGANI ZONDA C12 S

This car was designed by an Argentinian called Horacio Pagani. It is named after a wind that blows from the Andes mountains in Argentina. The Pagani Zonda is an exclusive supercar. There were only 15 built in the first year.

DID YOU KNOW?

When you buy a Zonda, you get a pair of driving shoes made by the Pope's shoe maker.

The Zonda looks like a fighter plane. It has a glass-roofed cabin, twin **spoilers** and a rocket-style exhaust. The inside is made of aluminium, suede, leather and carbon fibre.

STATS AND FACTS

LAUNCHED: *2001*

ORIGIN: *Italy*

ENGINE: *7,010 cc V12, mid-mounted*

MAX POWER: *419 kW (562 bhp) at 5,500 rpm*

MAX TORQUE: *749 Nm (552 ft lb) at 4,100 rpm*

MAX SPEED: *354 km/h (220 mph)*

ACCELERATION: *0–97 km/h (0–60 mph): 3.7 seconds*

WEIGHT: *1.25 tonnes*

COST: *£298,000*

The Zonda has no boot at all! The only luggage space is behind the seats.

This C12 S model has a massive 7.3 litre V12 engine. It is made by AMG, who make racing car engines for Mercedes-Benz.

PORSCHE 911 GT2

On the outside the GT2 looks like an ordinary Porsche 911 Turbo. But inside all of the luxuries have been removed to make the car drive like a racing car. There is harder **suspension**, a **rollcage**, special brakes and a lot of extra power! The GT2 costs £30,000 more than the Turbo, but it is the fastest 911 ever.

DID YOU KNOW?

The 2008 GT2 is the fastest road car in Porsche's history, capable of 329 km/h (204 mph).

The German car maker Porsche claim that the GT2 will accelerate to 300 km/h (186 mph) and brake to a stop in less than 60 seconds.

The rear wing and side panels have vents to cool the huge engine. There are also vents in the **nose** and slats in the bonnet. They direct air to cool the radiator and brakes.

STATS AND FACTS

LAUNCHED: *2001*

ORIGIN: *Germany*

ENGINE: *3,600 cc 24-valve turbo* Flat *6, rear-mounted*

MAX POWER: *339 kW (455 bhp) at 5,700 rpm*

MAX TORQUE: *622 Nm (459 ft lb) at 3,500 rpm*

MAX SPEED: *317 km/h (197 mph)*

ACCELERATION: *0–100 km/h (0–62 mph): 4.1 seconds*

WEIGHT: *1.44 tonnes*

COST: *£109,800*

The GT2 is 10 per cent more powerful and 7 per cent lighter than the 911 Turbo.

TVR TUSCAN

TVR are based in England. They have been making affordable sports cars for over 40 years. In 2000 the firm started selling the Tuscan. They made the car as light as possible and gave it a huge engine. The result is an amazingly fast car that costs far less than its rivals.

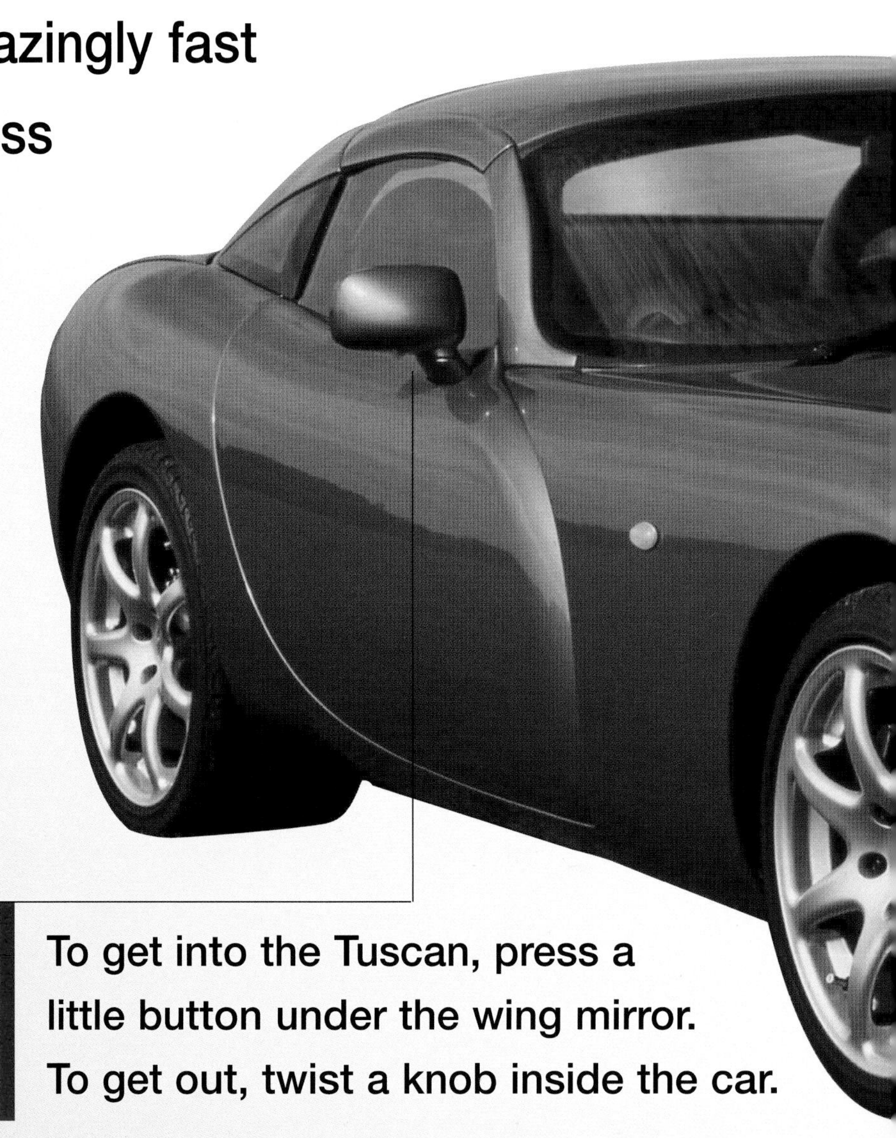

DID YOU KNOW?

John Travolta drove a purple Tuscan in the 2001 film Swordfish.

To get into the Tuscan, press a little button under the wing mirror. To get out, twist a knob inside the car.

The roof and the rear window can be taken off and stored in the Tuscan's large boot. There is even enough space left over for a couple of suitcases!

STATS AND FACTS

LAUNCHED: *2000*

ORIGIN: *UK*

ENGINE: *3,605 cc 24-valve* **Inline** *6, front-mounted*

MAX POWER: *261 kW (350 bhp) at 7,200 rpm*

MAX TORQUE: *393 Nm (290 ft lb) at 5,500 rpm*

MAX SPEED: *290 km/h (180 mph)*

ACCELERATION: *0–97 km/h (0–60 mph): 4.4 seconds*

WEIGHT: *1.1 tonnes*

COST: *£39,850*

The Tuscan's engine uses most of the space under the bonnet. It powers the car to 290 km/h (180 mph).

AIRBUS A380

Ever since the first plane took to the skies, aircraft have got bigger and bigger. In 1970 the American firm Boeing produced the enormous 747. In 2005, a new giant started flying: the enormous Airbus A380. It was built by the European company, Airbus.

DID YOU KNOW?

The A380-800F* freighter *is used to carry heavy loads. It carries up to 147 tonnes of cargo.

The body of the A380 is deeper and wider than a 747. There are two engines on each **wing**.

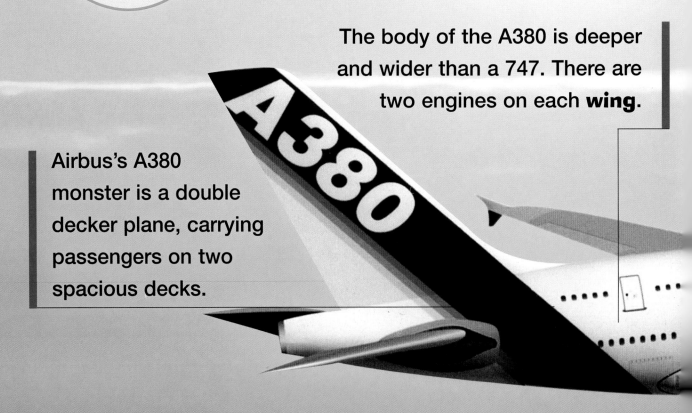

Airbus's A380 monster is a double decker plane, carrying passengers on two spacious decks.

The standard A380 has room for 555 passengers, travelling in economy, business and first classes. However seating is flexible, and some airlines might choose all-economy seating, and carry around 800 people.

STATS AND FACTS

LAUNCHED: *2005*

ORIGIN: *Europe*

MODELS: *Five passenger versions, and the A380-800F for cargo*

ENGINES: *Four Rolls-Royce Trent 900 engines providing 356 kN (36,280 kg) thrust or four Engine Alliance GP7000 turbofans, rated at 311 kN (31,713 kg) thrust*

WINGSPAN: *79.8 metres (262 feet)*

LENGTH: *73 metres (240 feet)*

COCKPIT CREW: *Two*

SEATING: *Up to 853*

MAX SPEED: *1,020 km/h (634 mph)*

MAX WEIGHT: *590 tonnes*

RANGE: *15,092 km (5,378 miles)*

LOAD: *Up to 800 passengers or 150 tonnes of cargo*

COST: *£154 million*

SR-71 BLACKBIRD

In 1960 the USSR shot down a US spy plane. After this disaster the American military were ordered to make a craft that would never be shot down again. The result was the amazing SR-71, packed with cameras and **sensors**. In 20 years of dangerous missions, no Blackbird was ever lost in combat.

DID YOU KNOW?

The Blackbird once flew from New York to London in 1 hour 55 minutes.

The Blackbird was made in top secrecy. President Lyndon Johnson refused to admit that it even existed until 1964.

STATS AND FACTS

LAUNCHED: *1962*

ORIGIN: *USA*

MODELS: *SR-71A, SR-71B and SR-71C*

ENGINES: *Two Pratt & Whitney J58-P-10s with* **afterburners**, *each providing 144.4 kN (14,724 kg) thrust*

WINGSPAN: *16.94 metres (55.6 feet)*

LENGTH: *31.65 metres (104 feet)*

COCKPIT CREW: *Two*

MAX SPEED: *3,621 km/h (2,250 mph) (Mach 3.4)*

MAX WEIGHT: *78 tonnes*

RANGE: *4,828 km (3,000 miles)*

LOAD: *Sensors and powerful cameras*

COST: *£33 million*

Each engine has enough **thrust** to power an ocean liner. The large spikes catch air to keep the plane balanced in flight.

The SR-71's **airframe** is made of a special material called **titanium alloy**. It protects the planes from the extreme heat produced when flying at such high speeds.

B-2 SPIRIT

Stealth technology has developed very quickly. By 1978 it was possible to design an aircraft that was almost invisible to **radar**. One of the most striking of these planes was the B-2. The first model flew in July 1989, and looked like it came from another planet.

The B-2's skin is jet black and smooth. All the joints are carefully concealed.

The B-2 is really just a giant wing with sharp edges. The strange bulges hide the plane's engines, **cockpit** and bombs.

The plane has just two crew on board. The rest of the cockpit is taken up by computer-controlled flight equipment.

STATS AND FACTS

LAUNCHED: *1989*

ORIGIN: *USA*

MODELS: *The US Air Force has 20 planes, all slightly different*

ENGINES: *Four General Electric F118-GE-110 turbofans each rated at 84.5 kN (8,618 kg) thrust*

WINGSPAN: *52.43 metres (172 feet)*

LENGTH: *21.03 metres (69 feet)*

COCKPIT CREW: *Two*

MAX SPEED: *1,014 km/h (630 mph)*

MAX WEIGHT: *181.4 tonnes*

RANGE: *12,302 km (7,644 miles)*

LOAD: *Up to 22.6 tonnes of many types of nuclear or conventional bombs, missiles or mines*

COST: *£1.6 billion (in 1998)*

The B-2 is stuffed full of computers and heat and noise reducing technology. It is the world's most expensive aircraft. In 1998 each plane cost an amazing £1.6 billion!

B-52 STRATOFORTRESS

After World War II, the US Air Force decided to create huge aircraft that would put people off starting wars. They were called the B-52 Stratofortresses, and were monster eight-engined jet bombers. In 1952 the first of these giants took to the skies.

DID YOU KNOW?

There are six ejection seats on a B-52 in case of emergency.

The B-52 has sensors that let the plane fly very close to the ground during combat missions.

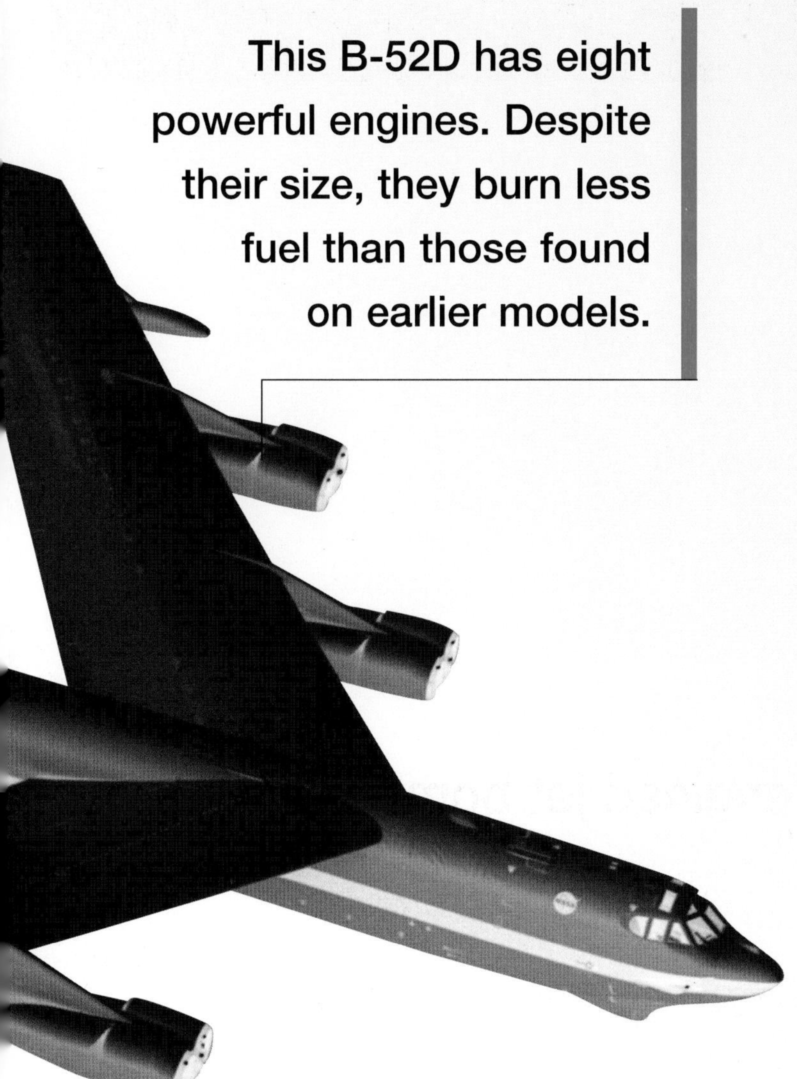

This B-52D has eight powerful engines. Despite their size, they burn less fuel than those found on earlier models.

STATS AND FACTS

LAUNCHED: *1952*

ORIGIN: *USA*

MODELS: *XB-52, YB-52 (1952), B-52A to B-52H (1954–65)*

ENGINES: *Eight 75 kN (7,711 kg) thrust Pratt & Whitney TF33 turbofans*

WINGSPAN: *56.39 metres (185 feet)*

LENGTH: *49.05 metres (161 feet)*

COCKPIT CREW: *Six*

MAX SPEED: *958 km/h (595 mph)*

MAX WEIGHT: *256.7 tonnes*

RANGE: *20,223 km (12,566 miles)*

LOAD: *Nuclear or high-explosive bombs, cruise missiles and a variety of guns*

COST: *£6 million*

This B-52 is being refuelled in flight. **Air refuelling** allows B-52s to fly almost anywhere in the world.

EUROFIGHTER TYPHOON

European countries get together to develop new warplanes. For each partner this is cheaper than developing an aircraft by themselves. The latest example is the Typhoon, developed by Britain, Germany, Italy and Spain.

DID YOU KNOW?

The idea for a Eurofighter dates back to 1979. However, it was over 20 years before the first Typhoon was built.

Only 15 per cent of the outside of the Eurofighter's body is made of metal. The rest is mainly lightweight carbon fibre that lets it cruise at great speeds without overheating.

The Typhoon has two engines. It also has a large triangular wing and small powered **foreplanes** on each side of the nose. The Typhoon comes in one or two seat versions.

STATS AND FACTS

LAUNCHED: *2002*

ORIGIN: *Europe*

MODELS: *Single seat and two seat versions*

ENGINES: *Two Eurojet EJ200 reheated turbofans each providing 89 kN (9,072 kg) thrust*

WINGSPAN: *10.95 metres (36 feet)*

LENGTH: *15.96 metres (52.4 feet)*

COCKPIT CREW: *One or two*

MAX SPEED: *2,129 km/h (1,323 mph) (Mach 2)*

MAX WEIGHT: *21 tonnes*

RANGE: *2,897 km/h (1,800 miles)*

LOAD: *One 27-mm gun (not used by UK) and up to 8 tonnes of missiles or bombs on 13 attachments*

COST: *£20 million*

The twin engines allow the Typhoon to accelerate to **Mach** 1 – the speed of sound – in under 30 seconds. The Typhoon can also take off in just five seconds!

F-117A NIGHTHAWK

First flown in 1981, the F-117A is perhaps the weirdest aircraft ever made. Its shape is designed to break up enemy radar signals. Because it can be air refuelled, the F-117A can travel almost anywhere in the world. This amazing plane was made by the US firm Lockheed Martin.

DID YOU KNOW?

The only non-black parts of the F-117A are the windows.

The F-117A is made up of hundreds of flat surfaces. These deflect enemy radar and make the plane almost invisible.

The F-117A is not really a fighter plane but a bomber. It carries its weapons inside, behind doors with zigzag edges. They open and shut very quickly to release bombs.

STATS AND FACTS

LAUNCHED: *1981*

ORIGIN: *USA*

MODELS: *Five prototypes and 59 production aircraft*

ENGINES: *Two General Electric F404-F1D2 special turbofans each giving 48 kN (4,899 kg) thrust*

WINGSPAN: *13.2 metres (43.3 feet)*

LENGTH: *20.08 metres (65.9 feet)*

COCKPIT REW: *One*

MAX SPEED: *1,127 km/h (700 mph) (Mach 1)*

MAX WEIGHT: *23.8 tonnes*

RANGE: *Without air refuelling about 2,414 km (1,500 miles)*

LOAD: *Usually two 907 kg laser-guided bombs*

COST: *£75 million*

There are four F-117As on display in the USA. One is on view to the public at the National Museum of the US Air Force. You can walk right up to this incredible plane.

HARRIER

By the end of the 1950s air forces started asking for planes that could operate from backyards, forest clearings or even small ships. To meet this need, Hawker Aircraft in England launched one of the first **VTOL** (Vertical Take-Off and Landing) aircraft in 1969. This plane was called the Harrier.

DID YOU KNOW?

The US Marine Corps use the Harrier to provide air power for a force invading an enemy shore.

This single-seater Sea Harrier operated from ships. There are also two-seater versions and trainer versions.

Harriers have a special system called **VIFF** (Vectoring in Forward Flight). It lets them perform impossible manoeuvres to confuse enemy fighter pilots.

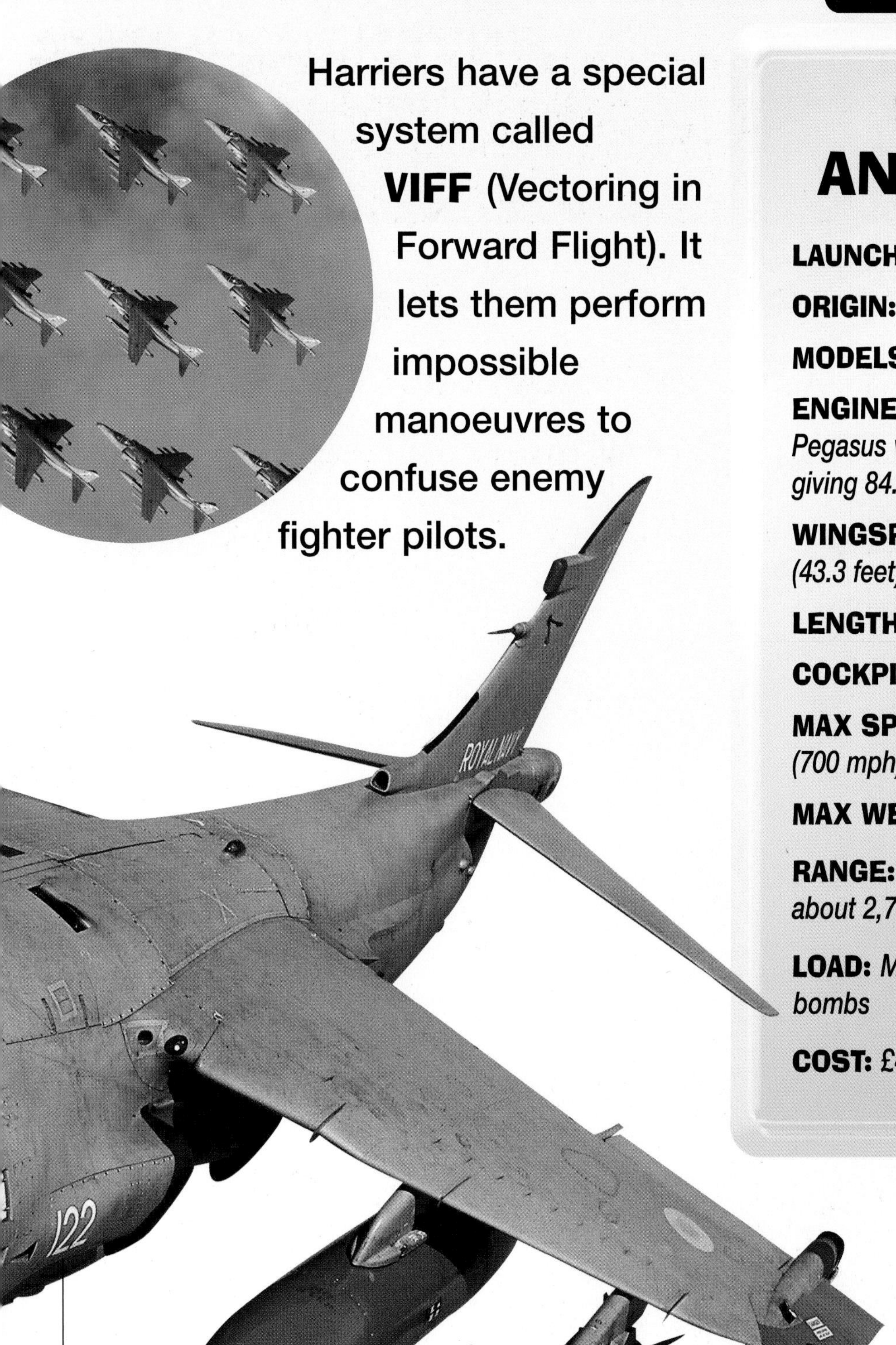

STATS AND FACTS

LAUNCHED: *1969*

ORIGIN: *UK*

MODELS: *Seven versions*

ENGINE: *One Rolls-Royce Pegasus vectored thrust turbofan giving 84.5 kN (8,618 kg) thrust*

WINGSPAN: *13.2 metres (43.3 feet)*

LENGTH: *14.1 metres (46.3 feet)*

COCKPIT CREW: *One or two*

MAX SPEED: *1,127 km/h (700 mph) (Mach 1)*

MAX WEIGHT: *14 tonnes*

RANGE: *Without air refuelling about 2,736 km (1,700 miles)*

LOAD: *Missiles, rockets and bombs*

COST: *£40 million*

The engine has two nozzles on each side. They blast to the rear for high speed; downwards for take-off or landing; or forwards to slow down.

JOINT STRIKE FIGHTER

In 1995 the US Air Force and Navy launched a programme for a JSF (Joint Strike Fighter). Their aim was to produce the next generation of advanced planes for airfields and aircraft carriers.

DID YOU KNOW?

In 2001 the F-35 entered into a 10-year system development and demonstration phase.

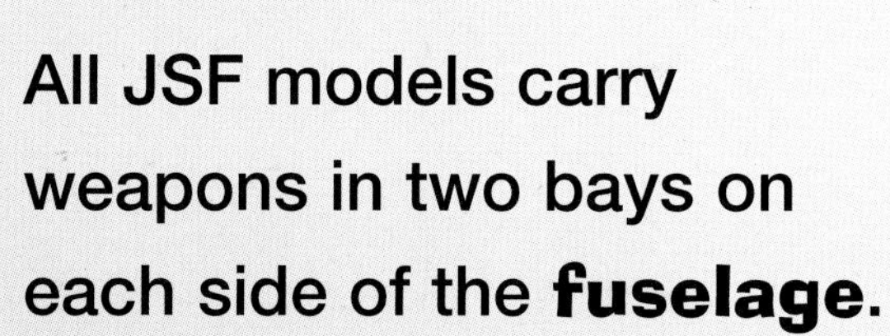

All JSF models carry weapons in two bays on each side of the **fuselage**.

The rear exhaust produces thrust to lift the aircraft. The F-35B is given extra lift by a fan that takes power from the engine.

STATS AND FACTS

LAUNCHED: *2006*

ORIGIN: *USA*

MODELS: *F-35A, F-35B and F-35C, described below*

ENGINES: *One Pratt & Whitney F135 turbofan delivering 178 kN (18,144 kg) thrust, with one Rolls-Royce Allison engine-driven lift fan on the F-35B*

WINGSPAN: *Up to 13.26 metres (43.5 feet)*

LENGTH: *15.39 metres (50.5 feet)*

COCKPIT CREW: *One*

MAX SPEED: *1,703 km/h (1,058 mph) (Mach 1.6)*

MAX WEIGHT: *27.2 tonnes*

RANGE: *About 2,221 km (1,380 miles)*

LOAD: *Enormous variety of guns, missiles and bombs up to 7.7 tonnes*

COST: *£66 million*

There are three versions of the JSF. The F-35A is the basic version. The F-35B comes with a more powerful engine. The F-35C *(left)* has a bigger wing, which can fold.

SPACE SHUTTLE

The first space flights relied on rockets – giant tubes which stood upright and were fired into orbit. In April 1981 the Shuttle was launched. It was the first spacecraft that could be brought back to Earth.

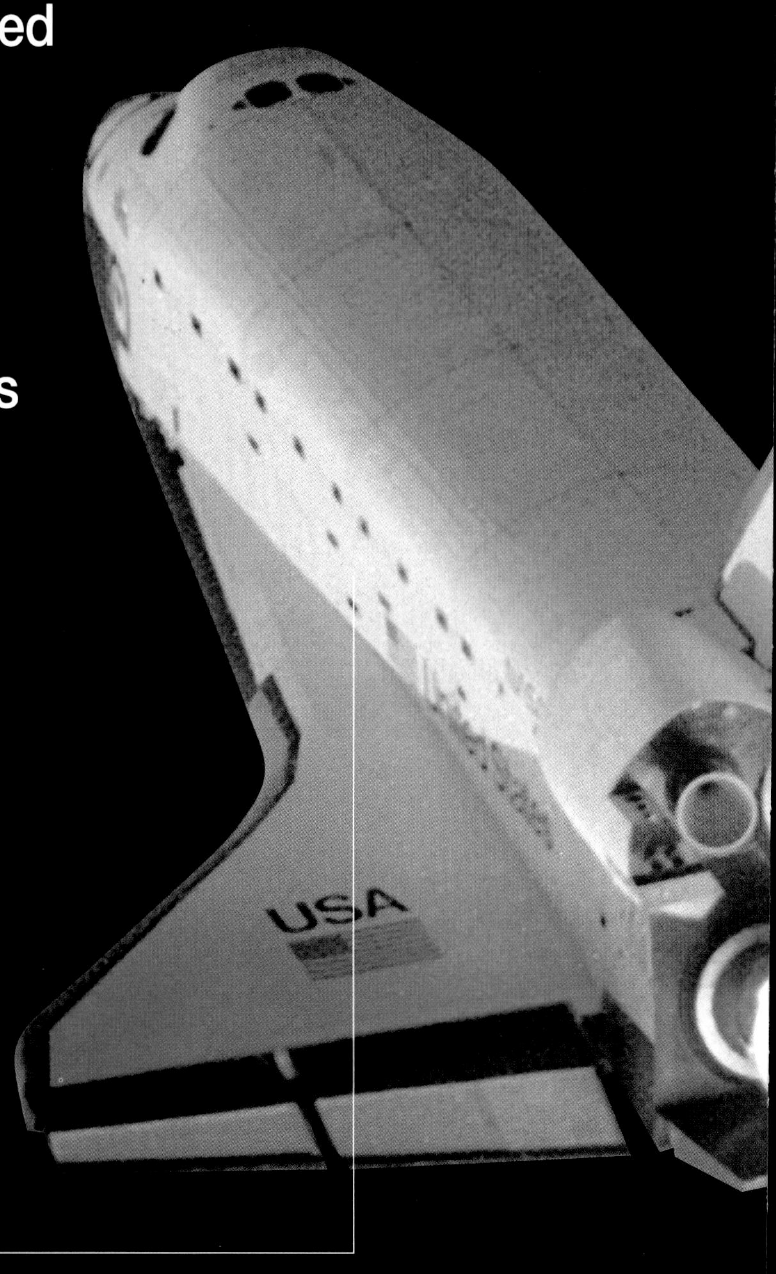

DID YOU KNOW?

The Shuttle's* boosters *fall off into the sea. They are recovered and used again.

At the front is an area for up to 10 crew, including two **pilots**. In the middle is a large **bay** for **satellites**. At the back are three big rocket **engines**.

Before launch, the **Orbiter** is fixed on a huge tank holding liquid oxygen and liquid hydrogen. Fixed on each side is a solid rocket **booster**.

STATS AND FACTS

LAUNCHED: *1981*

ORIGIN: *USA*

MODELS: *Enterprise, Columbia, Challenger, Discovery, Atlantis, Endeavour*

ENGINES: *Three orbiter engines with a combined thrust of 5,300 kN (540,000 kg), plus two solid-rocket boosters with a combined thrust of 25.6* **MN** *(2,610,000 kg)*

WINGSPAN: *23.79 metres (78.1 feet)*

LENGTH: *56.14 metres (184.2 feet)*

CREW: *Up to 10*

MAX SPEED: *28,066 km/h (17,440 mph)*

MAX WEIGHT: *2.041 tonnes*

RANGE: *187–649 km (116–403 miles)*

LOAD: *Satellites, components for the joint space station and space experiments*

COST: *£1.25 billion plus £294 million for each launch*

After the mission the Shuttle returns to Earth. It is protected by heat-resistant tiles. The Shuttle glides without engine power onto a runway, and is slowed down by a big **parachute**.

VOYAGER

On 23 December 1986 a strange looking airplane landed at Edwards Air Force Base, California. It had taken off from the same runway nine days previously and flown round the world non-stop. This had never been done before.

DID YOU KNOW?

During its epic journey,* Voyager *covered 40,211 km (24,986 miles) non-stop.

The *Voyager* was flown by two people. They had to lie down in a tiny space with a **propeller** at each end. The body of the plane was fixed on the centre of a fantastic wing.

Voyager was made from carbon fibre and **glass fibre**. At rest, its wings scraped on the ground, but in flight they curved upwards like the wings of a bird.

STATS AND FACTS

LAUNCHED: *1985*

ORIGIN: *USA*

MODELS: *One*

ENGINES: *Two Teledyne Continental engines – front 97 kW (130 bhp), rear 82 kW (110 bhp)*

WINGSPAN: *33.77 metres (110.8 ft)*

LENGTH: *8.9 metres (29.2 ft)*

CREW: *Two*

MAX SPEED: *196 km/h (122 mph)*

MAX WEIGHT: *4.4 tonnes*

RANGE: *44,185 km (27,455 miles)*

LOAD: *Two crew*

COST: *£1 million*

The *Voyager* was one of many weird looking airplanes created by Burt Rutan. It was flown around the world by his brother Dick *(right)*, with co-pilot Jeana Yeager.

X-43A

DID YOU KNOW?

Before the X-43A came the X-15. It reached an unbeaten speed of 7,297 km/h (4,534 mph) (Mach 6.87) during several flights.

NASA (National Aeronautics and Space Administration) is best known for making space rockets. It also carries out important research into aircraft. The X-43A is one of the latest research planes. It is used to find the best shape to fly at very high speeds in the upper part of the atmosphere.

The X-43A has a wide bottom, flat top and two fins. It is powered by a powerful **scramjet** engine, which burns hydrogen-based fuel.

After development, it is hoped that the X-43 will travel between Mach 7 and Mach 10, or 7,435–10,621 km/h (4,620–6,600 mph). This means it will be able to travel from London to New York in just 40 minutes, a journey that usually takes seven hours!

STATS AND FACTS

LAUNCHED: *2001 (test version)*

ORIGIN: *USA*

MODELS: *Three test models, each slightly different*

ENGINE: *GASL hydrogen-fuelled scramjet engine*

WINGSPAN: *1.5 metres (4.92 feet)*

LENGTH: *3.66 metres (12 feet)*

CREW: *Unmanned at present*

MAX SPEED: *10,621 km/h (6,600 mph) (Mach 10)*

MAX WEIGHT: *1.3 tonnes*

RANGE: *Unknown*

COST: *£250 million*

The X-43A's first flight took place on 2 June 2001. It was dropped from a B-52 over the Pacific Ocean. After the boosters ignited, the X-43A did not follow its set flight path and was deliberately destroyed. It was found that the booster's control system was to blame.

APRILIA TUONO FIGHTER

The Italian company Aprilia first became known as a maker of bicycles. Then, in 1968, they began producing motorcycles and mopeds. In 2003 Aprilia launched the Tuono Fighter. This used lots of the same parts as Aprilia's superbike the RSV Mille R, of which there were only ever 300 made.

DID YOU KNOW?

'Mille' is the Italian word for 'one thousand'. The RSV is called a 'Mille' because the engine is almost 1000 cc.

The Tuono Fighter has special **radial brakes** at the front. These are much stronger than normal brakes, so the bike can stop very quickly if it needs to.

One of the most eye-catching features of the Aprilia is its triple **headlight**.

STATS AND FACTS

LAUNCHED: *2003*

ORIGIN: *Italy*

ENGINE: *997.6 cc V-twin*

CYLINDERS: *2*

MAX POWER: *92 kW (123 bhp) at 9,500 rpm*

MAX TORQUE: *101 Nm (74.5 ft lb) at 7,400 rpm*

GEARS: *6*

DRY WEIGHT: *185 kg (408 lbs)*

MAX SPEED: *257.5 km/h (160 mph)*

FUEL TANK CAPACITY: *18 litres (4 gallons)*

COLOURS: *Red or grey (factory colours)*

COST: *£7,600*

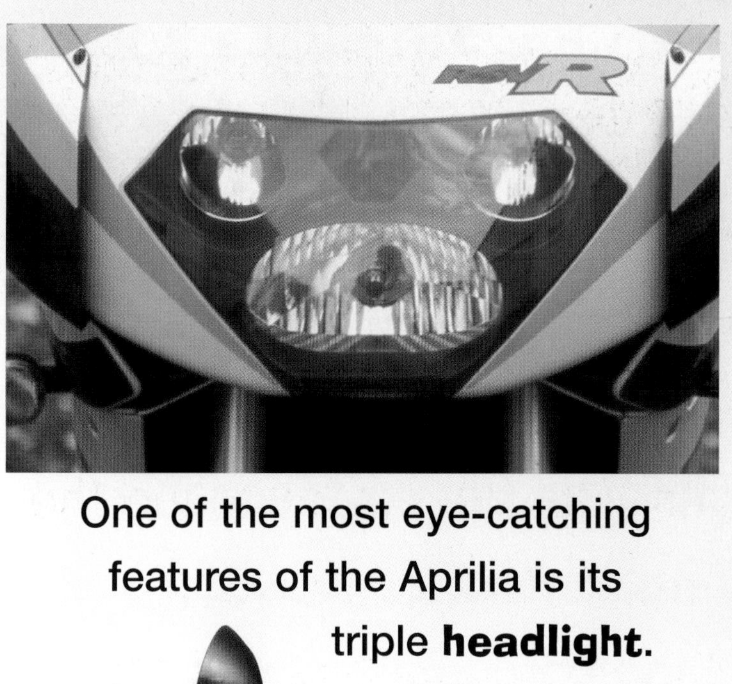

The Tuono is fitted with a steering damper, which helps the rider avoid wobbling when travelling at high speed.

BENELLI TORNADO

This Italian company was founded in 1911 by a widow called Teresa Benelli. She started the business to provide jobs for her six sons. The Benelli Mechanical Workshop started off making spare parts for cars and motorcycles. Then in 1921 the company made their first motorcycle. In 2002 Benelli started selling the Tornado, a 261 km/h (162 mph) superbike.

The Tornado's engine is also used as part of the bike's **frame**. This makes the bike stronger.

DID YOU KNOW?

The Benelli is built in Italy. But it was designed by an Englishman, and uses suspension made in Sweden.

The Tornado's radiator is under the seat. Two big **fans** suck in air to cool the radiator.

STATS AND FACTS

LAUNCHED: *2002*

ORIGIN: *Italy*

ENGINE: *898 cc*

CYLINDERS: *3*

MAX POWER: *110 kW (147 bhp) at 11,500 rpm*

MAX TORQUE: *100 Nm (73.8 ft lb) at 8,500 rpm*

GEARS: *6*

DRY WEIGHT: *185 kg (408 lbs)*

MAX SPEED: *261 km/h (162 mph) (estimated)*

FUEL TANK CAPACITY: *18 litres (4 gallons)*

COLOURS: *Green/silver*

COST: *£22,000*

A more powerful, racing version of the Tornado has competed at the Superbike World Championship. It was designed by Italian Ricardo Rosa, who has worked with the Italian car company Ferrari.

BUELL XB9R FIREBOLT

Buell was formed in 1993 by a man called Erik Buell. He set up the firm with help from Harley-Davidson, the famous American motorcycle company. Harley-Davidson are not known for making fast bikes. But Buell had the idea of using a Harley engine in a lighter bike to make a really fast machine.

DID YOU KNOW?

Weighing just 175 kg (386 lbs), the Firebolt is one of the lightest superbikes in the world.

The Firebolt has a belt instead of a chain to make the back wheel go round.

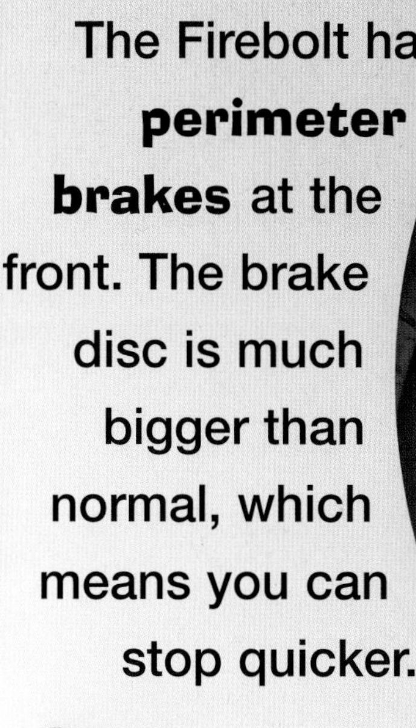

The Firebolt has **perimeter brakes** at the front. The brake disc is much bigger than normal, which means you can stop quicker.

STATS AND FACTS

LAUNCHED: *2002*

ORIGIN: *USA*

ENGINE: *984 cc*

CYLINDERS: *2*

MAX POWER: *68.6 kW (92 bhp) at 7,200 rpm*

MAX TORQUE: *92 Nm (67.9 ft lb) at 5,500 rpm*

GEARS: *5*

DRY WEIGHT: *175 kg (386 lbs)*

MAX SPEED: *209 km/h (130 mph) (estimated)*

FUEL TANK CAPACITY: *14 litres (3 gallons)*

COLOURS: *Arctic White, Battle Blue*

COST: *£7,345*

The Firebolt has several unusual features. The exhaust pipe, which is usually on the side of motorcycles, is underneath the Firebolt. The bike also has a hollow frame, which is used to store petrol.

CAGIVA V-RAPTOR 1000

The Cagiva company built their first two motorcycles in 1978. A year later, they were building over 40,000 bikes a year. This mad-looking machine was designed for the company by the Italian Miguel Galluzzi.

DID YOU KNOW?

The name Cagiva is made up of two letters each from the founder's surname and first name – Ca(stiglioni) Gi(ovanni) – and the first two letters of the company's hometown – Va(rese).

The Cagiva V-Raptor 1000 uses an engine made by the Japanese company Suzuki. The 'V' in the name describes the shape of the two **cylinders**.

This bike has claws! The V-Raptor has a strange set of talons by the passenger footrest.

STATS AND FACTS

LAUNCHED: *2000*

ORIGIN: *Italy*

ENGINE: *996 cc*

CYLINDERS: *2*

MAX POWER: *85 kW (114 bhp) at 8,500 rpm*

MAX TORQUE: *96 Nm (70.8 ft lb) at 7,000 rpm*

GEARS: *6*

DRY WEIGHT: *197 kg (434 lbs)*

MAX SPEED: *240 km/h (149 mph)*

FUEL TANK CAPACITY: *18 litres (4 gallons)*

COLOUR: *Red*

COST: *£7,149*

The bike is a 'naked' sportbike. This means that there is no **bodywork**, or **fairing**, covering the engine.

DUCATI 999R

DID YOU KNOW?

The 'R' is based on the same bike that is raced in the Superbike World Championships.

Ducati are an Italian motorbike company. The 999 comes in three versions – the 999, 999S and 999R. The 'R' is the fastest of the bikes, and is made of carbon fibre and aluminium.

This is a Ducati 749. It looks almost exactly the same as the 999, but it has a 749 cc engine. This means it has less power and is a bit slower.

The seat and fuel **tank** can be moved backwards and forwards, and the footrests can be moved up and down. This Ducati can be made comfortable to ride, however tall or short you are.

STATS AND FACTS

LAUNCHED: *2002*

ORIGIN: *Italy*

ENGINE: *999 cc*

CYLINDERS: *2*

MAX POWER: *104 kW (139 bhp) at 10,000 rpm*

MAX TORQUE: *108 Nm (79.7 ft lb) at 8,000 rpm*

GEARS: *6*

DRY WEIGHT: *193 kg (425 lbs)*

MAX SPEED: *281 km/h (175 mph) (estimated)*

FUEL TANK CAPACITY: *15.5 litres (3.4 gallons)*

COLOURS: *Red or yellow*

COST: *£19,300*

Each 999R has a unique silver badge to prove that it is a limited-edition bike.

HARLEY V-ROD

Famous for being the bikes that Hell's Angels like to ride, Harley-Davidsons have always been a bike for cruising on. There are lots of straight roads in America, and Harleys were made to ride long distances in comfort. However, the V-Rod is much sportier than other Harleys. It is the fastest bike the company have ever made.

DID YOU KNOW?

Despite being heavy motorcycles, the famous stunt rider Evel Knievel did all his jumps on a Harley-Davidson.

The V-Rod's fuel tank is under the seat. The space this saves leaves room for **air intakes**. These force more fuel into the bike's engine, supplying the V-Rod with extra power.

There is a special badge on the V-Rod's tank. It says that the Harley-Davidson company have been making bikes for over 100 years.

STATS AND FACTS

LAUNCHED: *2002*

ORIGIN: *USA*

ENGINE: *1,130 cc*

CYLINDERS: *2*

MAX POWER: *85.8 kW (115 bhp) at 8,000 rpm*

MAX TORQUE: *88 Nm (64.8 ft lb) at 6,300 rpm*

GEARS: *5*

DRY WEIGHT: *270 kg (590 lbs)*

MAX SPEED: *217 km/h (135 mph)*

FUEL TANK CAPACITY: *15.1 litres (3.3 gallons)*

COLOUR: *Anodized aluminium*

COST: *£13,995*

The V-Rod has a water-cooled engine. It was designed with the German sports car maker Porsche.

HONDA CBR1100XX BLACKBIRD

The Japanese company Honda are one of the biggest motorcycle makers in the world. The Blackbird used to be the fastest motorcycle in the world, until Suzuki built the Hayabusa. With a few tweaks, the Blackbird can rocket to an incredible 322 km/h (200 mph).

DID YOU KNOW?

In 2001, a rider on a turbo-charged Blackbird did a wheelie at an amazing 322 km/h (200 mph)!

The Blackbird has **linked brakes.** When you pull the front brake lever the back brake works too – and when you push the back brake pedal the front brake works as well.

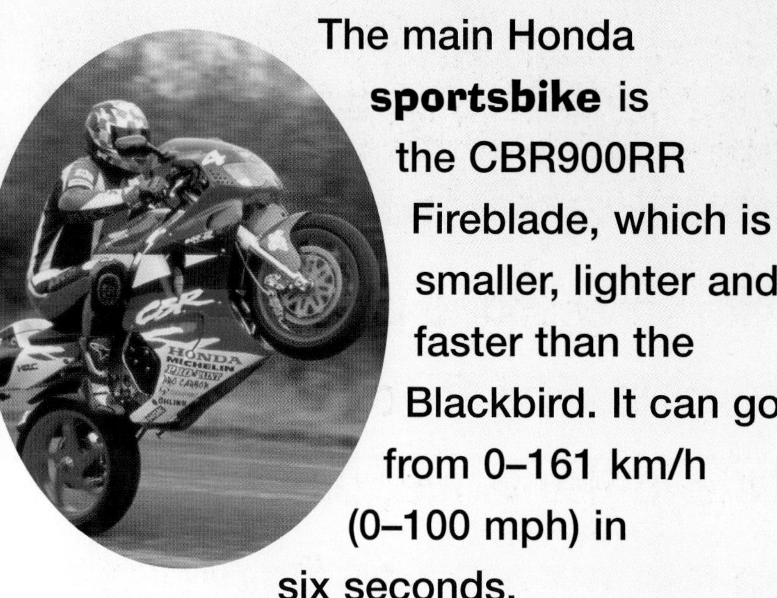

The main Honda **sportsbike** is the CBR900RR Fireblade, which is smaller, lighter and faster than the Blackbird. It can go from 0–161 km/h (0–100 mph) in six seconds.

STATS AND FACTS

LAUNCHED: *1996*

ORIGIN: *Japan*

ENGINE: *1,137 cc*

CYLINDERS: *4*

MAX POWER: *122 kW (164 bhp) at 9,200 rpm*

MAX TORQUE: *116 Nm (85.6 ft lb) at 7,300 rpm*

GEARS: *6*

DRY WEIGHT: *223 kg (492 lbs)*

MAX SPEED: *280 km/h (174 mph)*

FUEL TANK CAPACITY: *24 litres (5.3 gallons)*

COLOURS: *Black, blue, red*

COST: *£10,349*

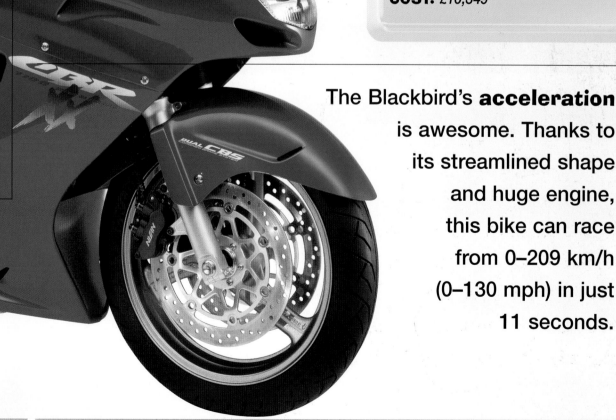

The Blackbird's **acceleration** is awesome. Thanks to its streamlined shape and huge engine, this bike can race from 0–209 km/h (0–130 mph) in just 11 seconds.

KAWASAKI NINJA ZX-12R

The Japanese company Kawasaki have always made very fast motorcycles. The ZX-12R is capable of just under 320 km/h (200 mph). The Ninja also has a big fuel **tank**, which means you can ride it long distances without stopping.

The ZX-12R has such good brakes that it is able to go from 113 km/h (70 mph) to a stop in under four seconds.

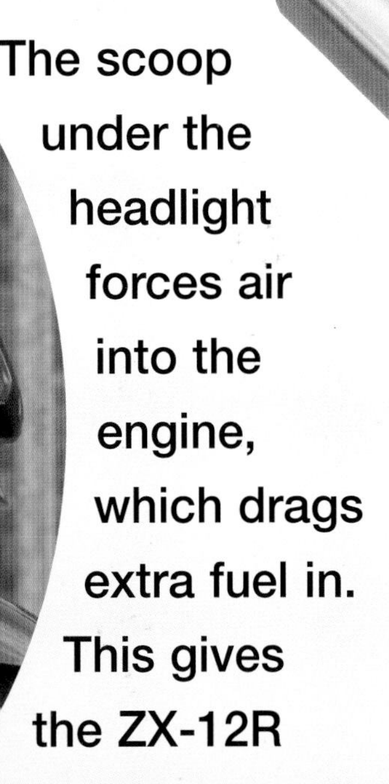

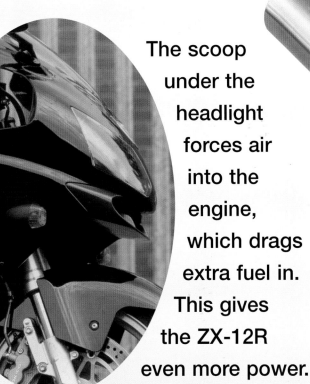

The scoop under the headlight forces air into the engine, which drags extra fuel in. This gives the ZX-12R even more power.

DID YOU KNOW?

From 2001 speed limiters were introduced that reduced the top speed of the ZX-12R to 300 km/h (186 mph).

STATS AND FACTS

LAUNCHED: *2000*

ORIGIN: *Japan*

ENGINE: *1,199 cc*

CYLINDERS: *4*

MAX POWER: *123 kW (165 bhp) at 9,800 rpm*

MAX TORQUE: *130 Nm (95.9 ft lb) at 7,800 rpm*

GEARS: *6*

DRY WEIGHT: *210 kg (463 lbs)*

MAX SPEED: *305 km/h (190 mph)*

FUEL TANK CAPACITY: *20 litres (4.4 gallons)*

COLOURS: *Black/gold, silver, Kawasaki Green*

COST: *£9,315*

The ZX-12R's fairing was made with help from Kawasaki's aircraft division. It was designed to make the bike as aerodynamic as possible.

MV AGUSTA F4 SPR SENNA

MV Agusta are another Italian company with a racing history. Agusta bikes won 270 Grand Prix between 1950–75 before the company ran out of money and closed. Then, in 1999, MV Agusta were brought back to life with the launch of the stunning F4. Lots of people think the Senna is the most beautiful bike in the world.

The Senna's exhausts come out under the seat, rather than at the side of the bike.

DID YOU KNOW?

Whenever a MV F4 SPR Senna was sold, some of the money was given to educate Brazilian children.

The Senna's twin headlights are arranged on top of each other. This makes the front of the bike more aerodynamic.

STATS AND FACTS

LAUNCHED: *2002*

ORIGIN: *Italy*

ENGINE: *749 cc*

CYLINDERS: *4*

MAX POWER: *104 kW (140 bhp) at 12,600 rpm*

MAX TORQUE: *81 Nm (59.7 ft lb) at 10,500 rpm*

GEARS: *6*

DRY WEIGHT: *188 kg (414 lbs)*

MAX SPEED: *285 km/h (177 mph)*

FUEL TANK CAPACITY: *20 litres (4.4 gallons)*

COLOURS: *Grey and red*

COST: *£17,350*

The Senna was made in memory of the famous Formula One racing driver Ayrton Senna. Only 300 were made.

SUZUKI GSX1300R HAYABUSA

The Japanese bike maker Suzuki was formed in 1952. In 1998 they built a new motorcycle called the Hayabusa. At the time, the Hayabusa was the fastest bike in the world. This monster's engine is actually bigger than those found in many cars.

DID YOU KNOW?

A Hayabusa is so powerful that it can wear out a back tyre in as little as 1,600 km (1,000 miles).

The GSXR100 is the smaller brother of the Hayabusa.

The top speed is the same as the Hayabusa, but this bike has better acceleration because it is lighter.

The British land speed record for a motorcycle is held by a turbo-charged Hayabusa. This bike reached a speed of 414.3 km/h (257.4 mph)!

STATS AND FACTS

LAUNCHED: *1998*

ORIGIN: *Japan*

ENGINE: *1,298 cc*

CYLINDERS: *4*

MAX POWER: *116 kW (155 bhp) at 9,000 rpm*

MAX TORQUE: *134 Nm (98.8 ft lb) at 6,800 rpm*

GEARS: *6*

DRY WEIGHT: *215 kg (474 lbs)*

MAX SPEED: *299 km/h (186 mph)*

FUEL TANK CAPACITY: *18 litres (4 gallons)*

COLOURS: *Blue and black, blue and silver, silver*

COST: *£8,299*

The hayabusa is a Japanese bird of prey that eats blackbirds. Suzuki called their new superbike a Hayabusa because it is faster and more powerful than Honda's CBR1100XX Blackbird, its main rival.

YAMAHA YZF R1

The Yamaha Motor Company are one of the best known motorcycle producers in the world. Originally a maker of musical instruments, the firm started to make motorcycles after World War II. In 2002 Yamaha launched the latest version of their incredibly successful R1 bike, which has competed in the British Superbike Championship.

DID YOU KNOW?

The Yamaha R1 will do over 120 km/h (75 mph) in first gear, and over 160 km/h (100 mph) in second gear.

The R1 has no light bulbs at the back. Instead it is fitted with tiny **LEDs** (light emitting diodes). If one stops working, there are still another 20 providing light.

One of Yamaha's most popular bikes is the YZF-R6. It isn't as fast as an R1, but because it is small and light it can keep up with most bigger bikes on twisty racetracks and roads.

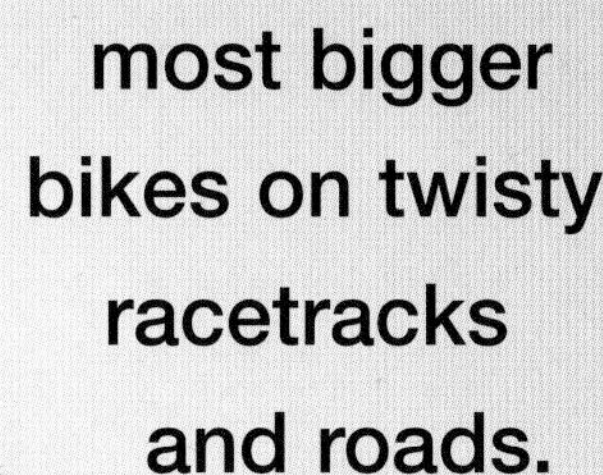

STATS AND FACTS

LAUNCHED: *1998*

ORIGIN: *Japan*

ENGINE: *998 cc*

CYLINDERS: *4*

MAX POWER: *113 kW (152 bhp) at 10,500 rpm*

MAX TORQUE: *107 Nm (79 ft lb) at 8,500 rpm*

GEARS: *6*

DRY WEIGHT: *174 kg (384 lbs)*

MAX SPEED: *283 km/h (176 mph)*

FUEL TANK CAPACITY: *18 litres (4 gallons)*

COLOURS: *Blue, red, white*

COST: *£9,134*

To make the new R1 even quicker, Yamaha have given it a lighter **chassis** and wheels. The front and back of the bike are also more pointed and aerodynamic.

CALIFORNIA QUAKE DRAG BOAT

The fastest racing boats on the water are drag boats. These single-seater craft surge like rockets at breathtaking speeds over the waves, often spending more time above the surface than on it. This incredible machine has reached speeds of about 370 km/h (230 mph)!

DID YOU KNOW?

Drag boat racing attracts crowds of up to one million people.

The *California Quake*'s 3,729 kW (5,000 **hp**) engine meant it became the first boat to race to 0.4 km (¼ mile) in under five seconds – a world record!

Bottled air is supplied to the pilot's helmet. This is so in the event of a crash, he can carry on breathing whilst waiting for divers to rescue him.

STATS AND FACTS

LAUNCHED: *1999*

ORIGIN: *USA*

ENGINE: *8,194 cc (500 cubic inch) nitromethane engine, generating 3,729 kW (5,000 hp)*

LENGTH: *7.62 metres (25 feet)*

WIDTH: *3.72 metres (12.2 feet)*

MAX SPEED: *198* **knots** *(370 km/h) (230 mph)*

MAX WEIGHT: *4.75 tonnes*

LOAD: *1 pilot*

FUEL CAPACITY: *20 litres (4.4 gallons)*

COST: *£60,000*

The most important part of the boat is the safety capsule. Complete with rollcage, it breaks free from the boat in the event of a high-speed crash.

DEEP FLIGHT SUBMERSIBLE

Submersibles are like miniature submarines. They are used for deep sea exploration. *Deep Flight I* is a tiny one-person submersible that does not use **buoyancy** (air/water) tanks. Instead it has short wings that let it 'fly' through the water.

The main body is made of a light material strong enough to resist the high pressure of water outside the submersible.

DID YOU KNOW?

A trip in a submersible down to the sunken wreck of the giant liner **Titanic** ***costs about £25,000.***

STATS AND FACTS

LAUNCHED: *1996*

ORIGIN: *USA*

ENGINES: *Two electric motors powered by ten 12 volt lead acid batteries, generating 4 kW (5 hp) each.*

LENGTH: *4 metres (13 feet)*

WIDTH: *2.4 metres (8 feet)*

MAX SPEED: *12 knots (22.2 km/h) (13.8 mph)*

MAX WEIGHT: *1.3 tonnes*

ASCENT RATE: *198 metres (650 feet) per minute*

DESCENT RATE: *150 metres (492 feet) per minute*

LOAD: *1 pilot*

COST: *£1 million*

Deep Flight I has a pair of stubby wings. Unlike the wings on a plane, though, these wings pull *Deep Flight I* down through the water instead of up off the ground.

Deep Flight I is equipped with up to four cameras and six lights. These are needed because the deep sea is totally dark.

ILLBRUCK RACING YACHT

Every year the fastest yachts in the world get together for the Round the World Yacht Race. In 2002 it was won by illbruck. The eight yachts in the competition covered over 59,500 km (37,000 miles) in total, taking almost nine months.

DID YOU KNOW?

The whole illbruck project – yacht, crew, back-up team, equipment, training, transport, supplies – cost nearly £16 million.

Round-the-world yachts battle giant waves, howling gales, collisions with icebergs and whales – and each other!

STATS AND FACTS

LAUNCHED: *2002*

ORIGIN: *Germany*

ENGINES: *n/a*

LENGTH: *19.5 metres (64 feet)*

WIDTH: *5.25 metres (17.2 feet)*

MAX SPEED: *36.75 knots (68km/h) (42 mph)*

MAX WEIGHT: *13.5 tonnes*

LOAD: *12 people*

COST: *£16 million (project cost)*

Crews pull the cables for the **sails** using high-speed **winches** with long handles. The height of the tallest mast is 26 metres (85 feet).

The *illbruck*'s satellite communications centre contains telephone, email and video transmission facilities.

JAHRE VIKING OIL SUPERTANKER

The biggest ships in the world are the giant tankers which carry crude oil, or petroleum. Their precious cargo is used to make petrol and other fuels, but also plastics, paints and hundreds of other products. These huge tankers are bigger than islands and take 8 kilometres (5 miles) to slow down and stop!

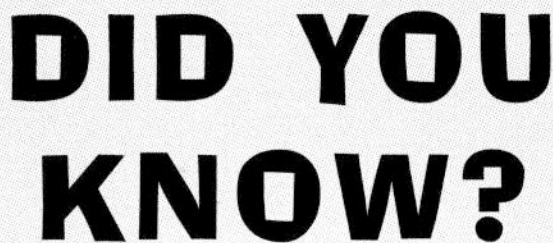

The* Jahre Viking *was bought in 2004 and renamed the* Knock Nevis. *It is now a permanently moored storage container.

Most of the ship is controlled by computer. The crew is usually about 35–40. They control the vessel and live in the comparatively small **stern** section of the ship.

Oil is pumped on board through pipes at the oil terminal or rig. It is pumped off again at a **refinery**.

STATS AND FACTS

LAUNCHED: *1979*

ORIGIN: *Japan*

ENGINES: *Four steam turbines each generating 37,300 kW (50,019 hp)*

LENGTH: *458 metres (1,500 feet)*

WIDTH: *69 metres (226 feet)*

MAX SPEED: *10 knots (18.5 km/h) (11.5 mph)*

MAX WEIGHT: *647,955 tonnes fully laden, 564,763 tonnes, unladen*

CREW: *35 to 40 people*

LOAD: *4,240,865 barrels of oil*

FUEL CAPACITY: *20,000 litres (4,400 gallons)*

COST: *£62.5 million*

The whole **deck** area can be as large as four football pitches. It can take several minutes to walk the length of the deck, so crew members sometimes use bicycles to get around!

JAMES CLARK ROSS RESEARCH SHIP

One of the world's toughest ships, the *James Clark Ross* can smash its way through ice more than two metres thick. This vessel is actually a huge floating laboratory, used for exploring and carrying out scientific research in the freezing seas of Anrctica.

There are five main sets of laboratories and science rooms on board the *James Clark Ross*. More can be loaded onto the deck, in house-sized containers.

JAMES CLARK ROSS

The main **hull** is extra-strong. It is made of very thick **steel**, capable of pushing through ice and fending off icebergs.

DID YOU KNOW?

A compressed air system prevents ice from squeezing and cracking the hull by rolling the ship from side-to-side.

STATS AND FACTS

LAUNCHED: *1990*

ORIGIN: *UK*

ENGINES: *Two Wartsilla R32 (3.1 MW each) and two Warsilla R22 (1.0 MW) engines delivering 6,340 kW (8,500 hp)*

LENGTH: *99 metres (325 feet)*

WIDTH: *18.85 metres (62 feet)*

MAX SPEED: *15.7 knots (29 km/h) (18 mph)*

MAX WEIGHT: *5,732 tonnes*

LOAD: *12 officers, 15 crew, 1 doctor, 31 scientists (maximum)*

FUEL CAPACITY: *1,350,000 litres (297,000 gallons)*

COST: *£37.5 million*

James Clark Ross surveys the oceans, and measures depths and currents. It also acts as a floating weather station, and even searches for strange creatures of the deep.

LOS ANGELES FIREBOAT NO. 2

Although ships are surrounded by water, they sometimes catch fire. Their engines and fuel may go up in flames, or they might carry a cargo like oil, which can burn. Almost every big port has fireboats on hand to tackle emergencies. This vessel is one of the Los Angeles Fire Department's five fireboats.

DID YOU KNOW?

Firefighters wear breathing kits. This is because some kinds of poisonous smoke can kill in just a few seconds.

All parts of the fireboat are flameproof, in case there is an explosion of burning fuel nearby.

When dockside buildings catch fire, it is time to call in the fireboats. As well as fighting ordinary fires, they can tackle electrical blazes by spraying special foam rather than water.

STATS AND FACTS

LAUNCHED: *1925*

ORIGIN: *USA*

ENGINES: *Two 522 kW (700 hp) V12 Cummins; three 283 kW (380 hp) six cylinder in-line Cummins; and two 391 kW (525 hp) V12 two cycle Detroits, plus six engines for pumps*

LENGTH: *30 metres (98.4 feet)*

WIDTH: *6 metres (20 feet)*

MAX SPEED: *17 knots (32 km/h) (19.6 mph)*

MAX WEIGHT: *152 tonnes*

LOAD: *14 crew*

FUEL CAPACITY: *9,801 litres (2,160 gallons)*

COST: *£135,550*

Six powerful diesel-powered **pumps**, all with their own engines, suck in water from around the boat. Then they fire out powerful **jets** of water from water-guns. These can reach heights of more than 150 metres (492 feet).

NIMITZ-CLASS AIRCRAFT CARRIER

DID YOU KNOW?

Up to 20,000 meals are served every day to hungry sailors on board the Nimitz.

Nimitz-class aircraft carriers are the biggest warships ever built. Each of these US giants is a floating army, navy and air force. The Nimitz-class has a crew the size of a small town, which includes 3,360 ships crew and 2,500 air crew. This number doesn't even include the soldiers and pilots!

This supercarrier carries up to 85 planes and six helicopters, along with all their spares, tools, pilots and service crew. Jet fuel is stored in swimming-pool-sized tanks.

Supercarriers like the Nimitz-class aircraft carrier are equipped with the latest computers, radar, missiles and other equipment. It takes three years to re-fuel, re-equip and re-fit these monsters.

STATS AND FACTS

LAUNCHED: *1972*

ORIGIN: *USA*

ENGINES: *Two nuclear reactors powering four steam turbines producing 194 MW (260,000 hp)*

LENGTH: *333 metres (1,093 feet)*

WIDTH: *40.8 metres (134 feet)*

MAX SPEED: *More than 30 knots (56 km/h) (35 mph)*

MAX WEIGHT: *Over 100,000 tonnes*

LOAD: *3,360 ships crew and 2,500 air crew*

COST: *£1.25 billion*

At 333 metres (1,093 feet), the Nimitz-class carrier is nearly as long as the Empire State Building is tall.

POLARIS VIRAGE TX JETSKI

The jetski is a combination of motorcycle, water-ski and snow-mobile. These vehicles are used for surging across the waves at great speeds. You can also do stunts on them, and even turn somersaults! If you lose your grip and fall off the craft, the water-jet stops immediately.

DID YOU KNOW?

The jetski was developed in the late 1960s. The idea came from US motorcycle rider Clay Jacobson who was working for the Kawasaki motorcycle company at the time.

The engine turns a fan-like **impeller**. This sucks in water through a large opening, and blasts it out the back as a fast, narrow **jet**.

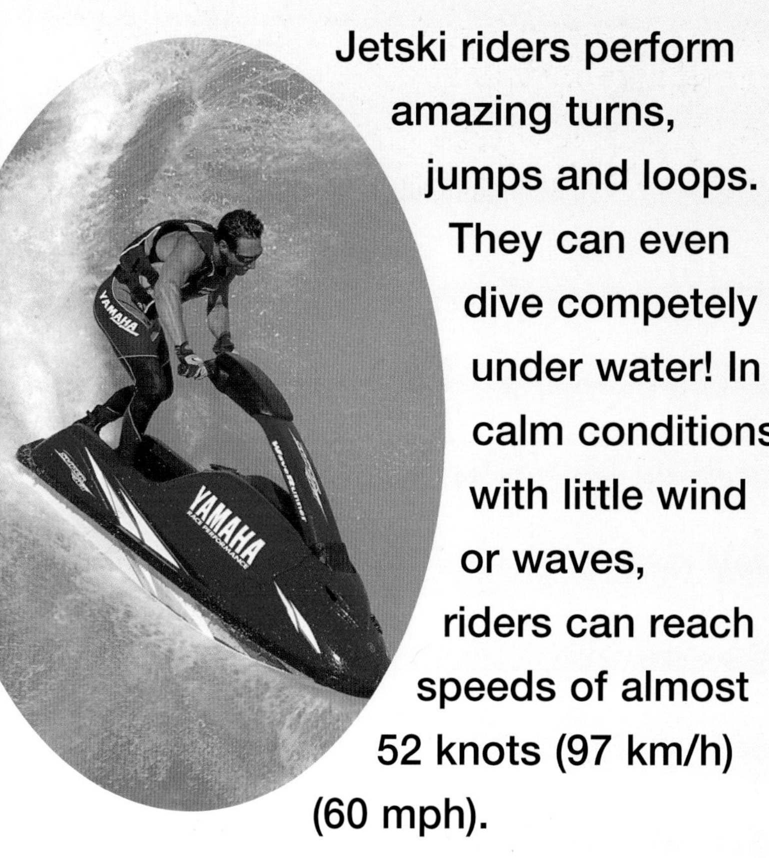

Jetski riders perform amazing turns, jumps and loops. They can even dive competely under water! In calm conditions, with little wind or waves, riders can reach speeds of almost 52 knots (97 km/h) (60 mph).

STATS AND FACTS

LAUNCHED: *2000*

ORIGIN: *USA*

ENGINE: *Polaris Marine 1200, producing 100 kW (135 hp)*

LENGTH: *3.06 metres (10 feet)*

WIDTH: *1.25 metres (4.1 feet)*

MAX SPEED: *52 knots (97 km/h) (60 mph)*

MAX WEIGHT: *285 kg (628 lb)*

LOAD: *1 pilot*

FUEL CAPACITY: *77 litres (17 gallons)*

COST: *Up to £8,000*

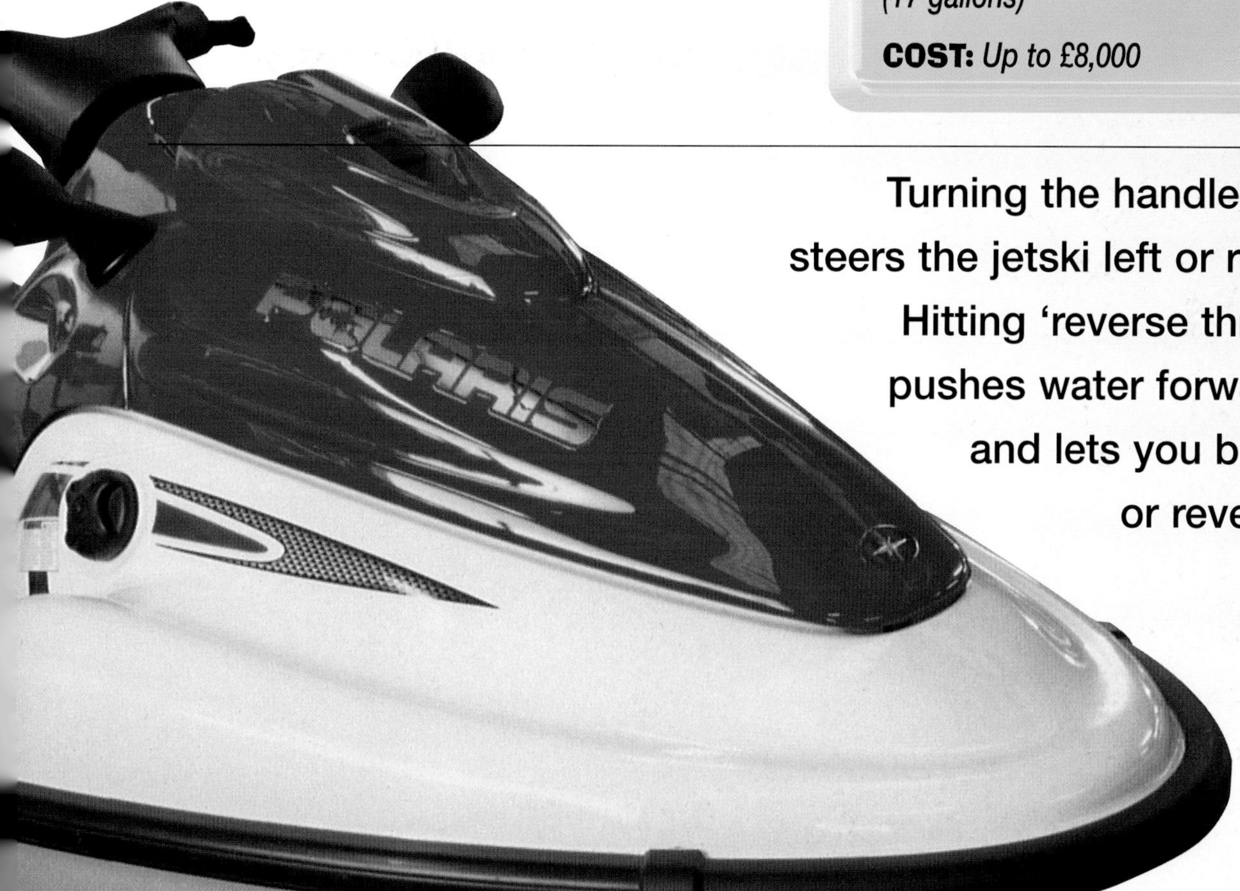

Turning the handlebars steers the jetski left or right. Hitting 'reverse thrust' pushes water forwards and lets you brake or reverse.

THE WORLD LUXURY LINER

The World is a luxury **liner** with a difference – you live on it! For a vast price you can buy a set of rooms on board to make your permanent home. The ship travels to exciting world events, including the Rio de Janeiro carnival in Brazil and the Formula One Motor Race in Monaco.

DID YOU KNOW?

Rental costs for an apartment on* The World *are between £1,400 and £3,500 ($2,000 and $5,000) per night.

The 12 decks have every luxury you can imagine. There are seven restaurants, a casino, a nightclub, theatres, gyms, tennis courts, swimming pools and cinemas.

On *The World*, people are not passengers, but residents on a lifetime's holiday. There are 110 main residences, plus 88 extra apartments which can be rented out to guests.

STATS AND FACTS

LAUNCHED: *2001*

ORIGIN: *Norway*

ENGINES: *Two Wartsila 12-cylinder diesels, generating 5,520 kW (7,402 hp)*

LENGTH: *196.35 metres (644 feet)*

WIDTH: *29.8 metres (98 feet)*

MAX SPEED: *18.5 knots (34 km/h) (21 mph)*

MAX WEIGHT: *43,524 tonnes*

LOAD: *Maximum of 976 residents, guests and crew*

FUEL CAPACITY: *1,150,000 litres (33,000 gallons)*

COST: *£164 million*

The hull of *The World* was built using giant pieces of steel, lifted into place using huge cranes.

TRENT CLASS LIFEBOAT

DID YOU KNOW?

In the seas around the UK, lifeboats are called out between 15 and 20 times a day.

Every sailor has two terrible fears – shipwreck and drowning at sea. Brave lifeboat crews are always ready for rescue missions, and their boats must stay safe, even in the worst storms. The powerful Trent class lifeboats are run by the UK's RNLI (Royal National Lifeboat Institute).

The hull of this lifeboat is made of various plastics, carbon fibres and other **composites**. Unlike metal these are very light but also very strong, and they never rust.

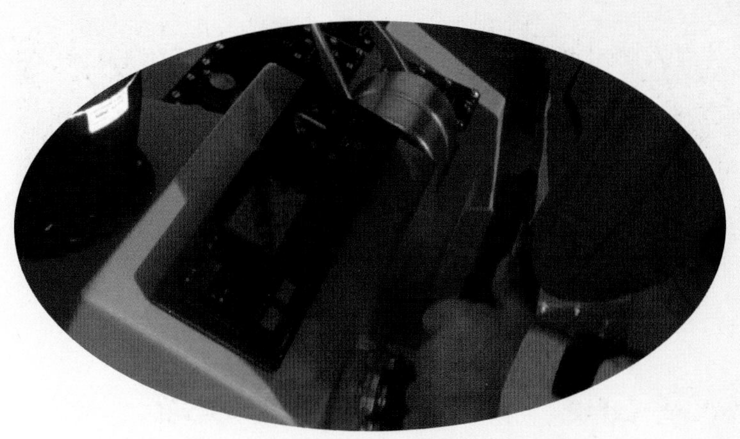

Special radar and radio equipment can track ships in distress. This technology uses the Marsat and Sarsat emergency satellite navigation systems.

STATS AND FACTS

LAUNCHED: *1994*

ORIGIN: *UK*

ENGINES: *Two MAN diesels, 603 kW (808 hp) per engine, each about as powerful as a Formula One racing car engine*

LENGTH: *14.26 metres (46.8 feet)*

MAX SPEED: *25 knots (47 km/h) (29 mph)*

MAX WEIGHT: *27.5 tonnes*

LOAD: *6 crew, plus 10 survivors*

FUEL CAPACITY: *4,100 litres (902 gallons)*

COST: *£1.25 million*

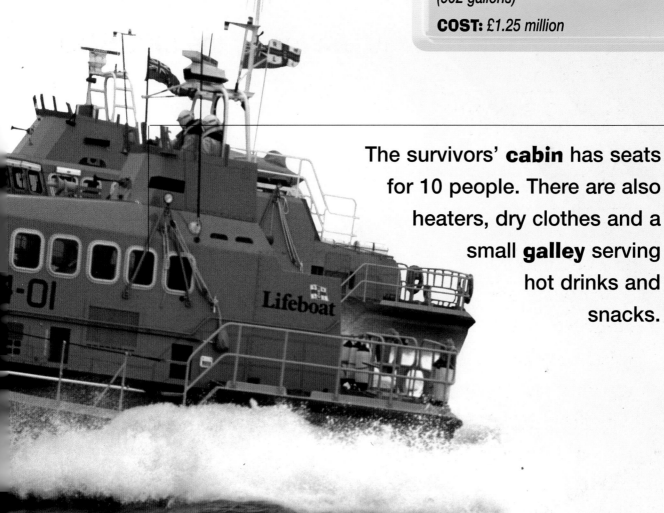

The survivors' **cabin** has seats for 10 people. There are also heaters, dry clothes and a small **galley** serving hot drinks and snacks.

GLOSSARY

Acceleration Making a vehicle go faster.
Aerodynamic A shape that cuts through the air around it.
Afterburner A system which injects extra fuel into the exhaust gases of a plane to provide large amounts of extra power.
Air intakes Large scoops that direct air into the engine, sucking in extra fuel to give a bike more power.
Air refuelling A method of refuelling military aircraft whilst in flight, via a fuel hose linked to a tanker aircraft.
Airframe The framework and covering of an aircraft.
Aluminium A lightweight, but strong, metal.
bhp (brake horse power) The usual measure of an engine's power.
Body The outer part of a car that covers the chassis and engine.
Bodywork The plastic panels which cover the chassis and engine of a car or motorcycle.
Booster Canister containing fuel that is attached to the side of a space rocket as it is launched.
Brakes The parts of a vehicle used to slow it down.
Buoyancy The upwards pushing force that water gives to objects, causing them to float if they are light enough.
Cabin An enclosed area on a ship, aircraft or spacecraft that holds the crew, passengers and cargo.
Carbon fibre A modern lightweight material used to make lots of types of vehicles.
cc Cubic capacity, the measurement used for the size of an engine.
Chassis The part which holds the engine, wheels and body of a car or motorcycle together.
Cockpit The part of an aircraft where the pilot and his assistants sit.
Composite A material or substance which is made of a mixture of materials, such as plastics, metals and fibre-glass. Composites are usually very light and very strong.
Convertible *See Roadster.*
Coupé A two-door hard top car.
Cylinders The parts of the engine where fuel is burned to make energy.
Dashboard The panel behind the steering wheel that usually contains the speedometer and other dials.
Deck The main floor or storey of a ship, and especially the uppermost flat area where people walk about.
Deployed Brought something into use.
Dynamic Stability Control A driver aid which can safely brake any or all four wheels.
Ejection seats Seats, usually fitted in military aircraft, that can be fired or ejected from the aircraft.
Engine The part of a vehicle where fuel is burned to create energy.
Exhausts Pipes at the back of a vehicle where poisonous gases (made when fuel is burned) are let out. In cars and bikes, the exhaust is also used to reduce engine noise.
Fairing The front and side parts of the bodywork.
Fans The parts of a bike that pushes or pulls cool air through the radiator, helping to cool the engine.
Foreplanes The moveable surfaces at the front of a plane that provide extra lift and balance.

Formula One A famous motor racing championship.
Four-wheel drive A car that has power delivered to all four wheels.
Frame The part of a motorcycle which holds the engine, wheels and bodywork together. Sometimes called the chassis.
Freighter An aircraft made to carry cargo rather than passengers.
ft lb (foot pound) A unit used to measure torque. A foot pound is the torque that is generated by one pound of force being applied at right angles to a pivoting lever arm one foot long.
Fuselage The central body of an aircraft.
Galley The kitchen or dining area on a ship.
Gearchange paddles The levers on a steering wheel used to change up and down gears.
Gears A system that lets a car or bike go faster or slower without damaging the engine.
Glass fibre A modern lightweight material used to make lots of types of vehicles.
Headlight The bright light at the front of the car or bike.
hp (horsepower) The measure of an engine's power, originally based on the power of an engine compared to a horse.
Hull The main part or body of a ship, which floats on the water.
Impeller A fan-shaped propeller or screw in a tube that sucks water through the tube.
Jet A stream of fluid forced out under pressure from a narrow opening or nozzle.
Jets The parts of an engine that provide the lifting power for an aircraft.
Knot One nautical mile per hour, equal to 1.85 kilometres per hour, or 1.15 miles per hour.
kN (kilonewton) Unit of force equal to 1000 newtons.
kW (kilowatt) Unit of power equal to 1000 Watts.
LEDs (light emitting diodes) the sources of light used in some brake lights.
Liner A large ship that carries passengers.
Linked brakes System where the front brake lever also works the back brake, and the back brake lever works the front brake.
Mach A measurement which relates the speed of an aircraft to the speed of sound. Mach 1 is the speed of sound (1,127 km/h or 700 mph) Mach 2 is twice the speed of sound.
MN (meganewton) Unit of force equal to 1,000,000 newtons.
Nose The front end of a car or an aircraft.
Nm (newton metre) A unit used to measure torque. A newton metre is the torque that is generated by one newton of force being applied at right angles to a pivoting lever arm one metre long.
Orbiter A spacecraft or satellite designed to orbit a planet or other body without landing on it.
Parachute A large canopy with a body harness underneath. It is designed to slow the rate of descent of a person from an aircraft.
Perimeter brakes A system where the brake disc is mounted round the edge of the wheel.
Pilots The people qualified to fly an aircraft, spaceship or boat.
Production car A standardized car which has been produced on a large-scale.
Propeller A machine with spinning blades that provides thrust to lift an aircraft.
Pumps Machines used for raising water or other liquids.
Radar A system using invisible radio waves, beamed out and reflected back by objects as 'echoes'. These are displayed on a screen to help identify other ships, planes, land, icebergs and similar items.
Radial Brakes A system where the brake discs are mounted at the bottom of the forks, parallel to the wheel.
Radiator A device through which water or other fluids flow to keep the engine cool.

Refinery A place where oil is turned into petrol.
Roadster A car with a roof that can be folded back or removed.
Rollcage A metal framework within some vehicles that prevents crushing in the event of it turning over in a crash.
rpm Revolutions (revs) of the engine per minute.
Sails Fabric spread to catch or deflect the wind as a means of propelling a ship or boat.
Satellite navigation A system which tells you where you are, using satellites in space.
Scramjet A hydrogen-fuelled engine designed for flying at five times the speed of sound.
Sensors Devices that help pilots fly their aircraft, detect enemy aircraft, or fire weapons accurately.
Spoilers The lightweight panels attached to a car to prevent the vehicle lifting up at high speeds.
Sportsbike A fast motorcycle that has been developed for road use.
Stealth technology The technology used to make a plane almost invisible.
Steel A very strong metal.
Stern The rear part of a ship or boat.
Submersibles Boats that can function when under water.
Superbike A fast motorcycle that is very similar to a race bike.
Supercar A fast, high performance sports car.
Suspension Springs and shock absorbers attached to the wheels of a car or bike, giving a smooth ride even on bumpy surfaces.

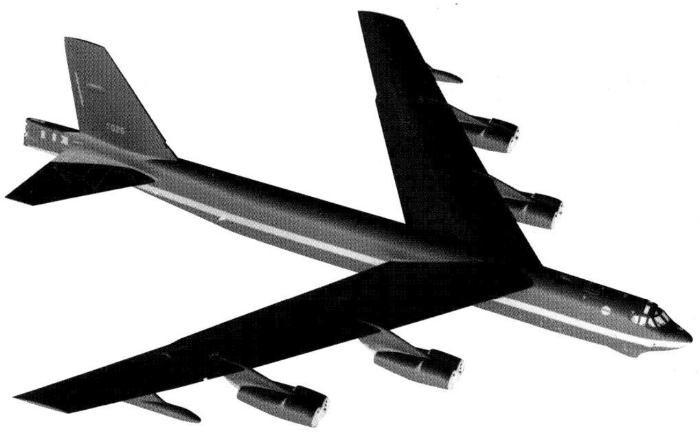

Tank A hollow metal unit where petrol is stored.
Targa A hard top car with a removable roof panel.
Thrust A pushing force created in a jet engine or rocket that gives aircraft enough speed to take off.
Titanium alloy A light, strong and heat-tolerant material.
Torque The force with which engine power can be delivered to a car or motorcycle's wheels.
Turbo A system that increases a vehicle's power by forcing more air into the engine.
Tyre A rubber covering for a wheel, filled with compressed air.
V/Inline/flat The arrangement of the cylinders in an engine.
V8/V12 The engine size given in number of cylinders.
Valve A device that controls the flow of petrol into the engine.
VIFF Vectoring in Forward Flight. System that lets a plane change direction very suddenly.
VTOL Vertical Take-Off and Landing. System that holds an aircraft in the air as it takes off or lands.
Winches A system that lifts something by winding a line around a reel.
Wings The part of an aircraft that provides lift, placed on either side of the fuselage.
Wingspan The distance between the tips of the wings of an aircraft.

INDEX

INDEX